Tornado

Perspectives on Tornado Disasters

Ben Hubbard

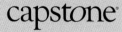

T0052466

Edited by Andrew Farrow, James Benefield, and Claire Throp
Designed by Philippa Jenkins
Original illustrations © Capstone Global Library Ltd 2014
Picture research by Tracy Cummins
Originated by Capstone Global Library Ltd

Library of Congress Cataloging-in-Publication Data
Hubbard, Ben, author.
  Tornado : perspectives on tornado disasters / Ben Hubbard.
    pages cm.—(Disaster dossiers)
  Summary: "What is it like to witness a tornado? This book looks at the Moore, El Reno, and other tornadoes, using firsthand accounts to describe events and people's experiences, providing multiple perspectives from eyewitnesses, survivors, the emergency services, scientists, and the media."—Provided by publisher.
  Includes bibliographical references and index.
  ISBN 978-1-4846-0183-9 (hb)—ISBN 978-1-4846-0189-1 (pb) 1. Tornadoes—Juvenile literature. 2. Survival—Juvenile literature. 3. Disaster relief—Juvenile literature. I. Title.

  HV635.5.H83 2015
  551.55'3—dc23   2013041160

Acknowledgments
We would like to thank the following for permission to reproduce photographs: Alamy pp. 25 (© epa european pressphoto agency b.v.), 28 (© James Pratt); AP Photo pp. 15, 21, 48 (Sue Ogrocki), 16 (The World-Herald/Chris Machian), 18 (The Oklahoman/Jim Beckel), 22 (Alonzo Adams), 24 (Brennan Linsley), 46 (The Daily Oklahoman/Paul B. Southerland); Corbis pp. 23 (© ED ZURGA/epa), 37 (© Jim Reed); Defense Imagery p. 14 (SFC Kendall James); Getty Images pp. 8 (Shane Keyser/Kansas City Star/MCT), 13, 34, 35 (DigitalGlobe), 39 (AFP/ ADRIAN DENNIS), 40 (David L. Nelson/AFP), 42 (Tom Pennington), 44 (JEWEL SAMAD/AFP); NOAA p. 11 (James Murnan); Science Source pp. 4 (Howard Bluestein), 31 (Jim Reed).

Cover photograph of a tornado forming a supercell in Nebraska reproduced with permission of Alamy (© RGB Ventures LLC dba Superstock).

Every effort has been made to contact copyright holders of material reproduced in this book. Any omissions will be rectified in subsequent printings if notice is given to the publisher.

Disclaimer
All the Internet addresses (URLs) given in this book were valid at the time of going to press. However, due to the dynamic nature of the Internet, some addresses may have changed, or sites may have changed or ceased to exist since publication. While the author and publisher regret any inconvenience this may cause readers, no responsibility for any such changes can be accepted by either the author or the publisher.

Printed and bound in the United States of America.
010678RP

Contents

Some words are printed in bold, **like this**. You can find out what they mean by looking in the glossary.

DOSSIER:
THE OKLAHOMA TORNADOES

In May 2013, an outbreak of deadly tornadoes tore through the state of Oklahoma. The outbreak included two rare EF5 tornadoes, the most powerful and destructive tornadoes on Earth. One of these tornadoes carved a 14-mile (22.5-kilometer) path of destruction through the densely populated suburb of Moore. In just 40 minutes, it reduced thousands of homes to rubble, flattened two schools, and killed 24 people. Only 11 days later, the widest tornado in U.S. history struck the area around the small city of El Reno. Nine people were killed as a result of the tornado's 296-mile (476-kilometer) per hour winds, the second-fastest winds to be recorded on Earth.

An approaching tornado is said to sound like a loud rumbling train or a whooshing waterfall.

∨

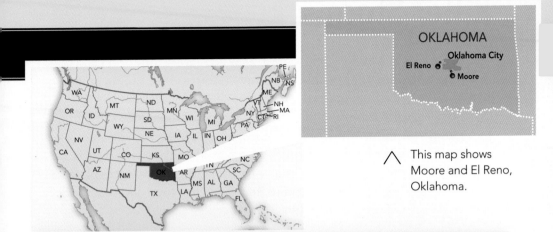

This map shows Moore and El Reno, Oklahoma.

QUICK FACTS

LENGTH OF MOORE AND EL RENO TORNADOES:	Lasted for around 40 minutes
CASUALTIES:	33 killed, over 300 injured
TOTAL COST:	Over $2 billion
PATH OF MOORE TORNADO:	Similar to another EF5 that struck in 1999 and an EF4 tornado that struck in 2003

OKLAHOMA TORNADO TIMELINE

MAY 13
The National Weather Service (NWS) issues a severe weather outlook for the central United States

MAY 16–18
Thunderstorm and tornado outbreaks batter Texas, Nebraska, Kansas, and Colorado

MAY 19
Tornadoes touch down in Oklahoma, killing two in the town of Shawnee and injuring 39

MAY 20
An EF5 tornado destroys schools and thousands of homes in the suburb of Moore, leaving 24 dead

MAY 31
The widest EF5 tornado in U.S. history strikes El Reno, Oklahoma, killing nine people

Killer Storms

The tornadoes that struck Oklahoma in May 2013 were terrifying examples of Earth's most violent atmospheric storms. A tornado is a rapidly spinning **funnel** of air that stretches from the bottom of a thunderstorm to the ground. Inside the funnel, wind speeds of up to 300 miles (483 kilometers) per hour give a tornado the suction power of a giant vacuum cleaner. Once a tornado has touched the ground, it travels at great speeds and sucks up anything in its path. During the Oklahoma tornadoes, trees were snapped like twigs, cars were picked up and tossed down like toys, and thousands of homes were smashed into splinters.

Unusual Oklahoma

Oklahoma experiences dozens of tornadoes every year, but the Moore tornado was different. This is because the tornado struck an area where many people lived. "Strong tornadoes occur pretty much every year. But most of them occur out in open, flat areas, or areas where there aren't many people. It's rare that we get one of these going through a major populated area," **National Severe Storms Laboratory (NSSL)** scientist Christopher Karstens told *National Geographic* magazine.

It was also rare that two EF5 tornadoes should occur within 11 days of each other. An EF5 on the **Enhanced Fujita Scale** is the strongest type of tornado and causes the greatest amount of damage (see the table on page 7). Tornadoes of this strength are unusual—there have been only nine EF5 tornadoes in Oklahoma since 1950. Incredibly, two of these EF5 tornadoes have struck Moore in virtually the same place.

A tornado is born

Tornadoes form inside the clouds of large thunderstorms. Thunderstorms are created when warm, humid air rises from the ground. As this warm air cools in the atmosphere, it forms into large, towering thunderstorm clouds. Cold air then rushes in to replace the rising warm air, which in turn creates strong winds. If these winds rotate, a tornado can form. When falling water from the cloud mixes with dust and **debris** from the ground, the tornado's familiar black funnel shape becomes visible.

The Enhanced Fujita Scale

Rating	Wind speed	Expected damage
EF0	65–85 mi. (104–137 km) per hour	Minor damage: Branches broken off trees, parts of roofs peeled off
EF1	86–110 mi. (138–177 km) per hour	Moderate damage: Windows broken, mobile homes overturned
EF2	111–137 mi. (178–220 km) per hour	Considerable damage: Cars tossed, homes shifted off **foundations**
EF3	138–167 mi. (222–268 km) per hour	Severe damage: Significant damage to large buildings, parts of well-constructed homes destroyed
EF4	168–199 mi. (270–320 km) per hour	Extreme damage: Houses leveled, cars thrown significant distances
EF5	200+ mi. (322+ km) per hour	Incredible damage: Trees snapped, houses swept away, steel-reinforced concrete buildings critically damaged

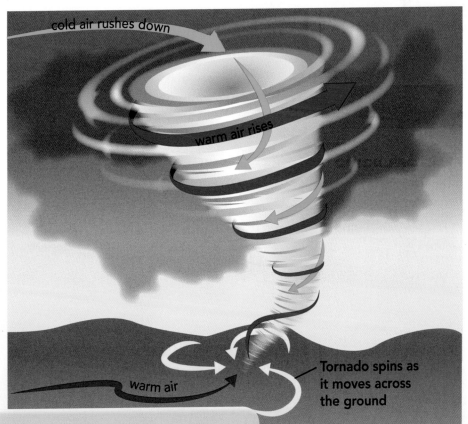

cold air rushes down

warm air rises

warm air

Tornado spins as it moves across the ground

A rotating tornado is formed when rising warm air (red arrow) meets with cold air coming down (blue arrows). The tornado then spins as it moves across the ground (yellow arrows).

Tornado Alley

Americans in "Tornado Alley" live in a unique geographical area. Here, warm, humid air from the Gulf of Mexico meets cold, dry air from Canada and mixes with hot, dry air from New Mexico and Arizona. When these air masses meet, they create the perfect conditions for tornadoes to form.

Of the approximately 1,250 tornadoes that hit the United States every year, over 400 form in Tornado Alley. These often occur from late winter to mid-summer, the period known as tornado season. However, **Storm Prediction Center (SPC) meteorologist** Roger Edwards warns: "Tornadoes can happen any time of year if the conditions are right!"

Being prepared

The people of Tornado Alley have to be prepared at all times. When thunderstorms gather overhead, they stay tuned to TV, radio, and online weather reports and prepare to take **shelter** if a tornado warning is issued. While many people have storm shelters and **safe rooms** built into their homes, others cannot afford them. Some residents reinforce their homes with "**hurricane clips**," which help secure the roof against high winds.

Often, this is enough—95 percent of all U.S. tornadoes have an EF3 rating or lower. But in Tornado Alley, over 25 percent of its annual tornadoes have a rating above EF3. The 138–167-mile (222–268-kilometer) per hour winds of an EF3 tornado can strip bark off trees and blow away homes with weak foundations. In an EF4 or EF5 tornado, all people can do is seek shelter and hope for the best.

On May 22, 2011, an EF5 tornado struck Joplin, Missouri, killing 158 people and injuring over 1,000 others.

Tornadoes around the world

Tornadoes don't just occur in the United States (page 38).

"Another area with similar conditions to Tornado Alley is Bangladesh. They have a lot of violent tornadoes. But a lot go unreported because they don't have nearly the observation network over there that we have over here."

Scientist Chris Weiss of Texas Tech University, speaking to *National Geographic* magazine

Practicing for a tornado

- Know where you can take shelter.
- Have a **weather radio** and cell phone handy for tornado alerts.
- Understand the difference between a tornado watch and warning (see page 10).
- Make sure you have mattresses and blankets nearby to protect against flying debris.
- If in doubt, "Get In, Get Down, Cover Up": get to the center of a building, get low, and cover yourself with blankets and coats.

SOUTH DAKOTA

NEBRASKA

COLORADO   KANSAS

OKLAHOMA

NEW MEXICO

TEXAS

■ Tornado Alley

Tornado Alley is situated in the southern **Great Plains** and stretches from South Dakota to Texas.

9

Tornado alerts

In the United States, the National Weather Service (NWS) issues tornado alerts. This is what each term means:

Tornado Watch
There is potential for tornadoes to form in the next four to eight hours. People should pay attention to the TV and radio, warn loved ones, and ensure access to shelter.

Tornado Warning
A tornado has been sighted or radar has shown a rotating, tornado-forming thunderstorm. Tornado sirens are sounded, and people typically have 13 minutes to find shelter.

Tornado Emergency
A confirmed tornado is expected to be strong and cause significant, widespread damage and numerous fatalities.

Sounding the storm sirens

On Monday morning, May 20, 2013, it became quickly obvious to NWS meteorologists that something big was about to happen. For three days, thunderstorms and tornadoes had battered the states of Tornado Alley. Then, on Sunday, May 19, a massive EF4 tornado killed two people in Shawnee, Oklahoma.

The NWS Storm Prediction Center in Norman, Oklahoma, was abuzz with activity. Phones rang nonstop, a radio crackled with storm chaser reports, and a team of meteorologists sat intently before computer screens, analyzing weather data. "When I came into the office it became obvious very, very quickly that the conditions were even more **volatile** than Sunday," Norman's NWS warning coordinator meteorologist Rick Smith told *Time* magazine.

The NWS meteorologists use every available source of information to help predict a tornado and warn the public. In addition to radar data, **satellite** images, and storm-analyzing computer programs, the meteorologists monitor Twitter and a weather service chat room used by TV stations and schools. Nine of the screens in the NWS Storm Prediction Center are kept tuned into the feed from TV news stations and weather helicopters.

Viewpoints from the ground

As conditions deteriorated in Oklahoma, helicopters and storm chasers sent video footage to television networks. Their footage provides live updates of what happens on the ground, so they have to get in close. Storm chasing is therefore both exciting and frightening at the same time. The Oklahoma storm chasers scanned radar images from their onboard laptops to figure out where a tornado might touch down. On May 20, storm chaser Bob Pack's laptop lit up with radar flashes of pink, orange, and red over Moore, Norman, and Newcastle. "This is not just going to be just an explosion. It's going to be a catastrophe," Pack told KBTX radio.

At 2:30 p.m., a huge thunderstorm cloud formed above Newcastle. As the cloud grew, a SkyNews9 helicopter sent in a concerned report:

"We're just rolled up on this storm…there is a lot of rotation in the cloud… We're about a mile and a half from it, and I can see it with my naked eye as it spins…there's nothing on the ground yet, but there's a lot of energy in this."

By 3 p.m., the NWS Storm Prediction Center team had seen enough. It issued the service's strongest alert: a Tornado Emergency. Sixteen minutes later, a tornado touched down near the small town of Newcastle.

Meteorologists at the NWS Storm Prediction Center in Norman, Oklahoma, analyze approaching storms.

In the Disaster Zone

Immediately after the NWS issued a Tornado Emergency for Moore, **storm sirens** screeched across the suburb. At that point, there was little the authorities could do except wait and keep their fingers crossed.

TIMELINE

1:10 p.m.
The NWS issues a Tornado Watch for 30 Oklahoma counties

1:56 p.m.
Spinning clouds are spotted above Oklahoma City

2:40 p.m.
The NWS issues a Tornado Warning for four Oklahoma counties

2:41 p.m.
The suburb of Moore sounds its 36 tornado sirens

2:56 p.m.
A tornado touches down 4.4 mi. (7 km) west of Newcastle. It quickly reaches Newcastle and develops an EF4 rating.

3:01 p.m.
The NWS issues a Tornado Emergency for Moore and Oklahoma City

3:03 p.m.
The tornado crosses **Interstate** 44 and destroys Celestial Acres horse farm, killing around 100 horses

3:16 p.m.
The tornado travels 5.5 mi. (8.8 km) to Briarwood School and strikes as a strengthened EF5. The roof is blown off and the walls collapse, but no one is killed.

3:18 p.m.
The tornado weakens to an EF4 and flattens the neighborhood of Penn Lane and Santa Fe Avenue. It then hits Plaza Towers Elementary school, killing seven students.

3:21 p.m.
The tornado devastates the second floor of Moore Medical Center and strikes Warren Theater. It then crosses Interstate 35, tossing cars into the central barrier.

3:35 p.m.
The tornado exits Moore, weakens to an EF1, and **dissipates**

Tweeting tornado viewpoints

As the tornado touched down, news channels, the NWS, and members of the public sent tweets, texts, and live reports about what was happening on the ground, from their perspective.

NWS, Norman, tweet, 3:03 p.m.
This is as serious as it gets for SW OKC and Moore. Please seek shelter now!

SkyNews9 Storm Chaser Val Castor, 3:13 p.m.
This is tearing up everything it hits. The air is full of debris. We're getting hit by debris here. This is a violent deadly tornado, please take cover now if you're in the path of this thing.

The Weather Channel live, reporter Kelly Cass, 3:20 p.m.
I think the [NWS] and Storm Prediction Center people are also worried about their loved ones. Some of them live in Moore, Oklahoma, and I bet it's hard for them to be working right now.

NWS, tweet, 3:22 p.m.
The tornado is so large now you may not realize it's a tornado. If you are in Moore, go to shelter NOW!

Emily Russell, Moore resident, tweet
Tornado skipped right over my house! My family is okay! Power is out and all I hear are sirens. Pray for Moore!

This NASA photograph shows the tornado's devastating path through Moore.

Get into your places

Principal Amy Simpson had just sixteen minutes between the tornado touching down and it striking her Plaza Towers Elementary School. As the tornado approached, thunderstorm clouds blackened the sky, hail pelted the school roof, and sirens wailed. Over the school's loudspeaker system, Simpson told everybody: "Get into your places." "They know exactly what that means. It means hallways, bathrooms, the safest places in the building," Simpson told NBC news.

As they learned in tornado drills, the students got onto their knees, put their heads up against walls, and used their hands and backpacks to cover their necks and heads.

The tornado tore the roof off the school and knocked down its walls. Children huddled together as their chairs were ripped into the air and wood, glass, and other debris rained down on their heads. Outside, a car was picked up from the parking lot and tossed down into the school's hallway. Then, just minutes later, the tornado passed.

Crosses on the Plaza Towers Elementary School fence serve as a memorial to the children who died in the tornado.

Searching the debris

The tornado left the school in ruins. Oklahoma Governor Mary Fallin described the view from a helicopter: "There's just sticks and bricks, basically. It was very **surreal** coming upon the school because there was no school."

As rescue workers pulled survivors from the wreckage, they called out their names over a megaphone. Terrified parents waited next door at St. Andrews United Methodist Church, hoping to hear their child's name. As families were reunited, tearful children recounted their experience. "A teacher took cover of us, Miss Crosswhite...she saved our lives," Damien Kline told ABC News.

But not everyone was so lucky. It soon emerged that seven children, all eight or nine years old, were killed.

The eye of the storm

Teacher Rhonda Crosswhite took shelter in a bathroom stall, covering kids' bodies with hers. She told ABC News:

"It just started coming down...it was like a freight train, and it felt like someone was beating me up from behind, because it was coming down onto my back."

Student Claire Gossett told *The New York Times*:

"It felt like the school was just flying."

Governor Mary Fallin surveys the damage from a helicopter.

15

On May 31, 2013, only 11 days after the EF5 tornado devastated Moore, the widest EF5 tornado recorded in the United States struck near the small city of El Reno, Oklahoma. Within minutes of touching ground, the tornado developed winds reaching 296 miles (476 kilometers) per hour as it tore through 16 miles (26 kilometers) of open countryside and across two major highways during rush-hour traffic. The NWS issued a Tornado Emergency for Oklahoma City, but, incredibly, the tornado missed the city and other densely populated areas. However, the thunderstorm responsible for the EF5 tornado sparked several smaller tornadoes and hail and caused **flash flooding** in the city.

This map shows the El Reno tornado's path, including its journey across Highway 81 and Interstate 40.

>

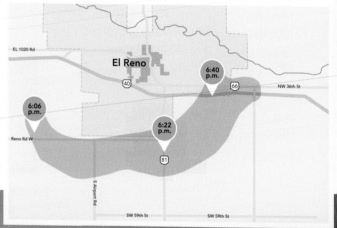

The El Reno tornado knocked down power lines.

∨

EL RENO TIMELINE

1:30 p.m.
The NWS issues a "particularly dangerous situation" (PDS) Tornado Watch. A PDS warning is reserved for situations that are likely to lead to extremely violent tornadoes. No tornado had been sighted by this time.

5:36 p.m.
The NWS issues a Tornado Warning for El Reno

6:06 p.m.
A large tornado touches down southwest of El Reno

6:22 p.m.
The tornado crosses Highway 81. A Doppler on Wheels unit (see pages 36–37) on the highway records wind speeds of 296 mi. (476 km) per hour.

6:40 p.m.
The tornado crosses Interstate 40, tossing cars into the air as it goes. It then dissipates.

7:10–8:00 p.m.
Smaller tornadoes are reported around Oklahoma City

8:00–9:00 p.m.
Flooding is reported on roads and parts of Oklahoma City

Highway horror

As the El Reno tornado bore down on I-40, the interstate highway, there was little drivers could do to get out of its path. Normally at 6:30 p.m., this road is busy with rush-hour traffic. But on May 31, many drivers fleeing the tornado were also using the road. The result was complete **gridlock**—vehicles were trapped with no way of escaping.

When the tornado hit I-40, it blew cars off the road, flipped over trucks, and demolished buildings by the roadside. Dozens were injured, and a mother and child were killed. "Their car was sucked up into the tornado and they were sucked out of their vehicle and thrown from [it]," Oklahoma Highway Patrol Trooper Betsy Randolph told ABC News.

As the tornado passed, heavy rain and hail pelted down on the wreckage on I-40. If the road had been less busy, more people would have escaped unharmed. The question was soon asked: "Why were they in their cars trying to outrun a tornado?"

"Vehicles are notorious as death traps in tornadoes because they are easily tossed or destroyed," says NWS meteorologist Roger Edwards.

Should I drive or should I hide?

The NWS gives the following advice for driving away from a tornado, which should only be done if "you do not feel safe from a tornado where you are":

- If you need to drive to find better shelter, do not wait to make the decision.
- If a Tornado Warning is in effect, it is too late to drive away safely!
- If you leave in your vehicle, know where you are going before you start the car.

Viewpoints from the road

There was a scene of panic and confusion on the roads that day. Some people left work early to take shelter at home. Others had followed advice from a TV meteorologist, who said on air: "If you can leave South Oklahoma City and go south, do it now." Some people, such as Moore resident Terri Black, wanted to avoid another devastating tornado. What Black found instead on I-40 was like a nightmare. "It was chaos. People were going southbound in the northbound lanes. Everybody was running for their lives. My car was actually lifted off the road and then set back down. The trees were leaning literally to the ground," she told Fox News.

In addition to being powerful and destructive, the El Reno tornado was highly unpredictable. It only stayed on I-40 for a few minutes, which meant most of those contributing to the congestion escaped with their lives. However, three storm chasers were not so lucky and died in their vehicles.

The highway patrol perspective

"I cannot stress to you just how important it is that if people don't have to be out, that they stay inside and seek shelter."

Highway Patrol Trooper Betsy Randolph

The Emergency Services React

Within 40 minutes, the Moore tornado had bulldozed its way through the suburb. Demolished buildings, crushed cars, and mountains of debris lay in its wake. Immediately, people's focus changed from surviving the tornado to urgently searching for survivors. The **National Guard**, police and fire departments, and **search and rescue teams** with sniffer dogs began hunting through the rubble for those trapped or injured. The local highway patrol set up a perimeter around the devastated areas, and **volunteers** were asked to stay away so the professionals could do their jobs. News and weather helicopters were kept out of the affected areas so that rescuers could hear cries for help. As the daylight began to fade, heavy lifting equipment and bright floodlights were brought in so that the search could continue through the night.

Rescuer stories: Heroes and heartbreak

On the morning of May 21, over 100 survivors had been found, and rescue crews expected to soon complete their search. "We will be through every damaged piece of property in this city at least three times. And we hope to be done by dark tonight," Moore Fire Chief Gary Bird told CNN.

Often the **first responders** called out to help in the search and rescue operation are locals themselves, such as National Guardsman Sergeant Warren Williams: "There are a lot of other agencies coming from other locations, but this is personal for us. These are people we know... so it's satisfying to be out here helping our fellow neighbors," Williams said on the U.S. Department of Defense web site.

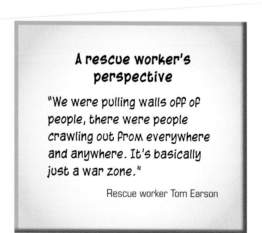

A rescue worker's perspective

"We were pulling walls off of people, there were people crawling out from everywhere and anywhere. It's basically just a war zone."

Rescue worker Tom Earson

Photographer Sue Ogrocki said she saw 12 children being pulled alive from the ruins of Plaza Towers Elementary School: "Police and firefighters used bars to try to lift a large chunk of a wall up as they pulled children out one-by-one from underneath. Parents and residents stood in a line helping to pass the children from one set of arms to another out of harm's way."

Local firefighter Russ Locke, who helped with the search at Plaza Towers Elementary School, described the heartbreak of finding the bodies of those who had not survived alongside those who had. "You have your own kids, and you want to find other people's kids and for it all to be OK. And sometimes it doesn't work out like that," Locke told *USA Today*.

What are search and rescue teams?

Urban search and rescue teams are the first responders used to locate, rescue, and offer medical support to victims trapped as a result of a disaster or emergency. Each team is made up of 31 specialists, four sniffer dogs, and equipment such as metal-cutting machines.

Rescue workers pull survivors from the rubble that was once Plaza Towers Elementary School.

Treating the injured

As survivors were pulled from the rubble of Plaza Towers Elementary School, they were passed down a human chain to the nearby Moore Medical Center. But the hospital had also been hit by the tornado and was dangerously unstable. Instead, survivors were given emergency treatment in the Warren Theater parking lot next door. Patients were then evacuated to nearby undamaged hospitals, which began treating the 387 people injured during the tornado. Off-duty doctors and nurses worked through the night. The wide range of injuries was mostly the result of flying **shrapnel**. "We've seen minor cuts and bruises to people coming in with **hypothermia** and open wounds…People have come here with pieces of wood in them," OU Medical Center Director Roxie Albrecht told the *Oklahoman* newspaper.

A pregnant mother's viewpoint

As the tornado demolished the second floor of the Moore Medical Center, Shay-la Taylor was inside giving birth. Her husband and child had been sent to a safer part of the hospital, but Taylor and her nurses stayed upstairs in the operating room. Taylor monitored the tornado's path on a smartphone

The injured are treated by Moore Medical Center workers.

Tornado-proof hospital

A week later, it was announced the remains of the Moore Medical Center had to be demolished. The story was familiar to those trapped inside St. John's Regional Medical Center in Joplin, Oklahoma, when an EF5 tornado devastated the building in 2011. The tornado blew the roof off the hospital and destroyed the backup generator, making electrical life-saving machines unable to function. Six people died during the tornado. A new tornado-proof hospital—Mercy Hospital Joplin—is planned to open in 2015. The hospital will feature buried electrical wiring to prevent power failure, shatter-proof windows, and a concrete slab roof that will be virtually impossible to blow off.

app, as nurses piled towels on top of her. Minutes later, the tornado struck. "The floor was shaking like an earthquake and then I saw the ceiling shaking too...Me and two of the nurses were all just holding hands and praying. My eyes were closed, but you could kind of see daylight. And I opened my eyes and I could see out the wall," Taylor told the Huffington Post. Incredibly, she was unharmed and gave birth to a baby boy. Hers was one of 11 babies born in Moore on May 20, 2013.

This is the parking lot of Moore Medical Center. Cars with an orange cross have been searched for occupants.

Aid, food, and shelter

By the end of May 22, all the missing people of Moore were accounted for, and those with injuries were being treated. After emergency crews checked for gas leaks and live electrical wires, residents were allowed to return to their homes. But many had no homes to return to. "It's crazy when you wake up and you don't have any clothes, you don't have any shoes, you don't have your toothpaste, you don't have nothing," Kristy Rushing told NewsOK. Rushing is one of around 3,000 Moore residents who lost everything in an instant.

Attention quickly turned to the basics—giving people food, shelter, and aid. The Oklahoma Department of Emergency Management coordinated the organizations providing services on the ground. The National Guard distributed 28,000 gallons (127,000 liters) of water and 30,000 meals within the first 48 hours. The Salvation Army opened three emergency canteens (mobile kitchens), and the Red Cross set up six shelters in community

Dawn breaks over the remains of a Moore home. The address has been drawn onto the door, so its owners can find it.

A charity mobile canteen gives out hot meals to tornado victims.

centers, churches, and university buildings. Telephone companies opened cell phone charging stations, with emergency phones and WiFi. Here, survivors could communicate with loved ones and register with the **Federal Emergency Management Agency (FEMA)** for recovery assistance. Health and safety workers inspected food vendors and shelters, and gave survivors and rescue workers **tetanus** vaccines against infected wounds.

What happens in less-developed countries?

When a natural disaster hits a major economic power such as the United States, help is usually at hand. However, in 2005, the U.S. government was heavily criticized for its delayed response in helping the victims of Hurricane Katrina. But what happens when a tornado hits a less economically developed country? On May 13, 1996, a tornado tore through Bangladesh, flattening 80 villages, killing 700 people, and injuring 33,000 others in under 30 minutes. The survivors criticized the government for reporting the number of casualties at only 22 and not sending relief for 24 hours. But despite the central government's inaction, local government authorities, volunteers from local communities, and charities immediately began treating the injured, feeding the survivors, and burying the dead.

DOSSIER:
DEADLY TORNADOES THROUGH TIME

Humans have only been recording tornadoes in depth for around 120 years. Here are some of the deadliest in modern times. For these tornadoes the Fujita scale was used, rather than the newer Enhanced Fujita scale.

QUICK FACTS CANADA, JUNE 30, 1912

LOCATION:	Regina, Saskatchewan
CASUALTIES:	28 killed, 300 injured
DAMAGE:	Over 500 buildings and houses destroyed
TOTAL COST:	$4.5 million
DISTANCE TRAVELED:	20 mi. (32 km)
INTENSITY:	F4–F5: 207–318 mi. (333–511 km) per hour winds

Although the cost of property damage was initially $1,200,000, it took Regina two years to rebuild and another 40 years to pay off its tornado debt.

QUICK FACTS UNITED STATES, MARCH 18, 1925

LOCATION:	Missouri, Illinois, Indiana
CASUALTIES:	695 killed, 2,027 injured
DAMAGE:	15,000 homes, 9 schools
DURATION:	3.5 hours
TOTAL COST:	$16.5 million
DISTANCE TRAVELED:	219 mi. (352 km)
INTENSITY:	F5: 261–318 mi. (420–511 km) per hour winds

The deadliest tornado in U.S. history and the longest ever recorded in the world, this "**Tri-State** Tornado" was actually just one of nine tornadoes that also struck the states of Kentucky, Tennessee, Alabama, and Kansas. Fifty-two additional lives were lost in the outbreak.

LOCATION:	Belyanitsky, Ivanovo, and Balino
CASUALTIES:	Over 400 killed, 213 injured
OUTBREAK:	8 or more tornadoes of F4–F5 intensity: 207–318 mi. (333–511 km) per hour winds
TOTAL AREA AFFECTED:	155,213 sq. mi. (402,000 sq. km)

The tornadoes reportedly swept away large industrial buildings, bridges, and cranes, peeled tarmac off the roads, and produced the world's heaviest hailstone, weighing 2.2 lbs. (1 kg).

QUICK FACTS ARGENTINA, JANUARY 10, 1973

LOCATION:	San Justo, Santa Fe
CASUALTIES:	54 killed, 350 injured
DAMAGE:	Over 500 homes
DURATION:	10 minutes
TOTAL COST:	US$60,000
DISTANCE TRAVELED:	300 yds. (275 m)
INTENSITY:	F5: 261–318 mi. (420–511 km) per hour winds

The tornado ripped grass from the ground, sucked a pond dry, threw vehicles hundreds of feet, and embedded a car in a concrete wall.

Telling the World

The Moore tornado made headlines both in the United States and abroad. For news providers, the impact of a natural disaster on people's lives has great appeal as a human-interest story. Because there were news teams already covering the buildup to the tornado, live footage of the tornado itself and the fallout afterward was immediately beamed around the world. In the United States, TV stations sent their top **news anchors** to report live from the scene. It was not long before they were joined by international news teams.

Live updates

Newspapers printed minute-by-minute updates on their websites. These reports included witness accounts, TV news clips, Twitter messages of support, and charity web site links. These kept people informed and enabled them to give **donations**. However, it all happened so quickly that when an incorrect fact was reported, it was often reported incorrectly worldwide.

Mixed reports

When the Oklahoma chief medical examiner reported that 51 people had died during the Moore tornado, the figure spread like wildfire. But many news providers used a different, incorrect figure. Then, less than 24 hours later, the medical examiner updated his own figure because some of the dead had been counted twice. This timeline shows how the number of dead was reported around the world.

News crews set up near the Moore Medical Center.

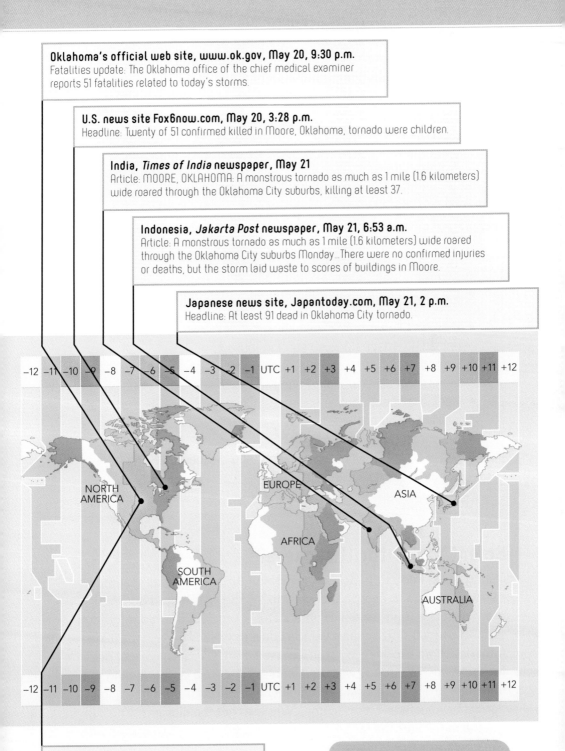

Oklahoma's official web site, www.ok.gov, May 20, 9:30 p.m.
Fatalities update: The Oklahoma office of the chief medical examiner reports 51 fatalities related to today's storms.

U.S. news site Fox6now.com, May 20, 3:28 p.m.
Headline: Twenty of 51 confirmed killed in Moore, Oklahoma, tornado were children.

India, *Times of India* newspaper, May 21
Article: MOORE, OKLAHOMA: A monstrous tornado as much as 1 mile (1.6 kilometers) wide roared through the Oklahoma City suburbs, killing at least 37.

Indonesia, *Jakarta Post* newspaper, May 21, 6:53 a.m.
Article: A monstrous tornado as much as 1 mile (1.6 kilometers) wide roared through the Oklahoma City suburbs Monday...There were no confirmed injuries or deaths, but the storm laid waste to scores of buildings in Moore.

Japanese news site, Japantoday.com, May 21, 2 p.m.
Headline: At least 91 dead in Oklahoma City tornado.

−12 −11 −10 −9 −8 −7 −6 −5 −4 −3 −2 −1 UTC +1 +2 +3 +4 +5 +6 +7 +8 +9 +10 +11 +12

NORTH
AMERICA

EUROPE

ASIA

AFRICA

SOUTH
AMERICA

AUSTRALIA

−12 −11 −10 −9 −8 −7 −6 −5 −4 −3 −2 −1 UTC +1 +2 +3 +4 +5 +6 +7 +8 +9 +10 +11 +12

Oklahoma's official web site, www.ok.gov, May 21, 4 p.m.
Fatalities update: The Oklahoma office of the chief medical examiner reports 24 fatalities related to Monday's storms.

This time-zone map shows how quickly one incorrect fact led to another after the tornado had struck.

Superstorm chasers

When news spread of a tornado outbreak in Oklahoma, storm chasers from across the United States jumped into their specially equipped vehicles and headed for the action. Some storm chasers are professionals who gather scientific data for research or film the tornado for television news. The NWS also has its own "storm spotters" who send it weather updates. But many of the storm chasers are **amateurs**, hoping to take video or photos of the storm. They upload the footage to YouTube and other Internet sites and can become famous. Many say the rise of social media web sites and reality TV programs such as *Storm Chasers* have encouraged more amateur storm chasers onto the road.

Storm chasing equipment

- Digital still cameras, video cameras, and webcams are used for uploading images and streaming footage.
- Laptop computers connect to the Internet via a cell phone to monitor weather updates and radar and to upload images.
- Radios, phones, police scanners, Citizens Band (CB) radio, and walkie-talkies are used.
- Advanced equipment can also include mobile **Doppler radar** (see pages 36–37), weather balloons, and devices that can be sucked into the tornado itself.

Scientists or thrill seekers?

During the El Reno tornado, congestion on the roads meant that many cars were unable to escape the tornado. All the NWS could do was tweet alerts for traffic to get off Interstates 40 and 35. But **radar** footage showed over 60 storm chaser vehicles driving *toward* the approaching tornado. Three experienced storm chasers were killed as a result. But for some, such a tragedy was predictable. "There's a strong feeling from veterans in the chasing community that the industry is heading in a dangerous direction…It's become, 'Who can get the closest? Who can get the most dramatic footage?'" meteorologist Jason Samenow told *National Geographic* magazine.

Others say professional storm chasers are essential, and that getting in close is a key element of their work. "Things like pressure and temperature and humidity—there's no other way to make these measurements other than to make measurements in the tornado itself. You need to be on the ground," University of Oklahoma professor Howard Bluestein told *National Geographic.*

Sheriff Gary Stanley of Woodward County, Oklahoma, also emphasizes the need for storm chasers. He said a storm chaser from a TV station spotted a tornado before it struck Woodward and saved lives by reporting it. "I'm glad we had storm chasers. We need storm chasers. But we don't need 200 of them," Stanley told the *Wall Street Journal.*

Storms chasers line the road in anticipation of a tornado.

The following accounts come from five of the Moore tornado survivors. They all found themselves in the path of the tornado when it struck the suburb on May 20, 2013.

Celestial Acres Thoroughbred Breeding and Training Center, 14200 S. Western Avenue, 3:03 p.m.

Horse-farm caretaker Lando Hite said he knew a tornado was close when everything went quiet. Seeing debris flying through the air, Hite set some horses free and took refuge in the stable. "I jumped in and it collapsed on top of me. It was unbearably loud, you could see stuff flying everywhere, just like in the movie *Twister*," Hite told KFOR News. Lando Hite survived the tornado, but the farm was destroyed, and around 100 horses were killed.

Briarwood Elementary School, 14901 Hudson Avenue, 3:16 p.m.

Teacher Ledonna Cobb was in her classroom when the tornado struck. Cobb used her body as a shield to protect students. "Once the roof came off the building, I felt myself being sucked and I knew if I was taken, all the little babies underneath me would be gone, too, so I just held on. I held on for dear life until the wall fell on top of me and knocked me out." Briarwood Elementary was flattened by the tornado, but there were no fatalities.

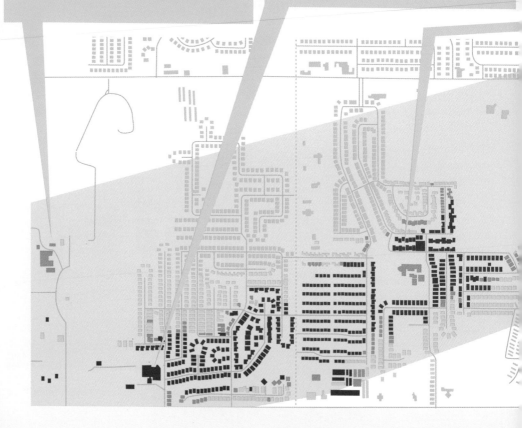

Elizabeth's House, Eagle & SW 11th Street, 3:18 p.m.

When Elizabeth heard about the tornado on her car radio, she sped back to the house to rescue her dog, Ginger. But as she opened her front door, she could see the tornado approaching. "I could actually see it and hear it roaring...I ran in the house, called the dog and the windows started busting through...I threw the pillows in the bathtub and said, 'Come on Ginger.' All I remember is hitting my head on the bathtub as it got picked up and thrown down," Elizabeth told KFOR News. Elizabeth and Ginger sustained minor injuries, but their house was destroyed.

Moore Medical Center, 700 S. Telephone Road, 3:21 p.m.

Dr. Stephanie Barnhart said workers moved patients into the safe area of Moore Medical Center and were treating them up until when the tornado hit the building. "The power went out and at that point we told the patients to get to the mattresses. We handed out blankets and sat on the floor and ducked for cover. It was very calm, amazingly...The weird thing was the area we were in—nothing was out of place. There was just a little dust." Although the tornado destroyed the second story of the Moore Medical Center, there were no deaths.

Warren Theater, 1000 Telephone Road, 3:21 p.m.

Amanda Danskin was inside the Warren Theater watching a movie when two members of the audience with iPhones announced a tornado was heading straight for them. Theater staff quickly ushered people into the foyer as the tornado struck. "There were some people crying and holding hands, and there was a feeling like this might be it, we might be done... The power went out, there was gusts of wind, and this roar, and it lasted for 5 or 6 seconds and then it was gone," Danskin told KJYO Radio. There were no injuries at the Warren Theater.

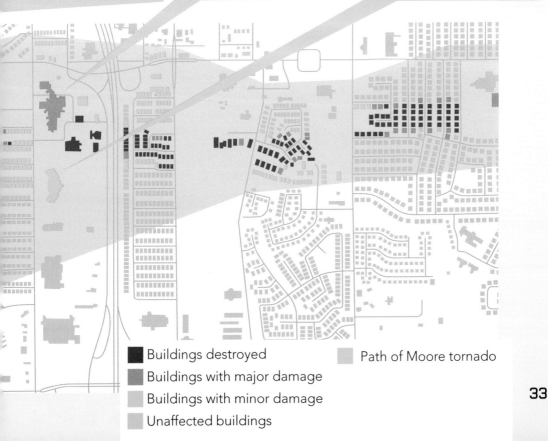

Buildings destroyed

Buildings with major damage

Buildings with minor damage

Unaffected buildings

Path of Moore tornado

33

Scientists at Work

As rescue workers searched for the survivors of the Moore tornado, scientists eagerly examined the ruined buildings to better understand it. In contrast to those just recovering from the disaster, the four NWS survey teams were excited to learn about the tornado's strength. "It's a bit like being a detective. You try to look at all the evidence and put together a puzzle of what you think happened as the tornado moved through," NWS meteorologist Todd Shea told the LiveScience web site.

The two-person survey teams photographed and documented evidence, such as the damage to buildings and how vehicles and other debris had been thrown around. They then compared this data to aerial pictures and a "damage indicator" computer program to estimate the tornado's strength.

The Moore tornado was given an initial EF rating of 4, but this changed when the survey teams reached Briarwood School. There, the amount of damage was consistent with a stronger tornado. By the afternoon of May 21, the survey teams completed their work, and the NWS officially upgraded the Moore tornado to an EF5. While the information made exciting headlines, it was of little comfort to the victims. For the meteorologists, however, it was extraordinary news. It meant the tornado was the second EF5 in the last 60

These photos show Moore before and after the EF5 tornado.

years to hit Moore. So why, within the large region of Tornado Alley, have such rare and violent tornadoes targeted such a tiny area?

Menacing Moore

According to Rick Smith, meteorologist at the NWS, the reason EF5 tornadoes have struck Moore so often is coincidence. "Scientifically, there is nothing special about Moore to cause tornadoes to happen there more than they happen anywhere else…it's just the way it's worked out. That seems weird, but there is no scientific explanation for it," Smith told the *Oklahoman* newspaper. Smith says that while scientists understand many things about tornadoes, they have only being studying them for 50 to 100 years, so some questions remain unanswered.

Tim Samaras, one of the storm chasers who died in the El Reno tornado, was well known for placing scientific equipment inside tornadoes to measure wind speeds. While these experiments aided tornado research, Samaras told *National Geographic* before he died that there was a lot to learn. "We still don't know why some thunderstorms create tornadoes while others don't. We're trying to collect as many observations as possible, both from outside and from the inside."

Forecasting heroes

Many heroes emerged during the Moore tornado. These included teachers who shielded students with their bodies and rescue workers who worked through the night to haul survivors from the rubble. But often, the unsung heroes of a tornado outbreak are those analyzing data behind computer screens—the meteorologists.

In 1925, there was no warning for the public of the Tri-State tornado, which caused the death of 695 people. By comparison, it is impossible to calculate the number of lives saved in 2013 as a result of the NWS's tornado alerts in Moore. "It is remarkable that only 24 people died in a city of tens of thousands. Experimental forecasts just 12 hours before the storm formed were remarkably accurate. They were able to pinpoint where the storms would begin that day and when," Center for Analysis and Prediction of Storms Director Kelvin Droegemeier told the National Science Foundation web site.

After the Tri-State tornado, it became obvious the United States needed a tornado warning system. The first tornado forecasting began in 1943 and was boosted by the introduction of radar in the 1950s. Between the 1960s and 1990s, radar was used alongside computers to produce the tornado forecasting systems used today.

Tornado forecasting today

Modern weather forecasters use a combination of Doppler radar, satellite images, and computer analysis programs to make life-saving tornado predictions. To spot tornado-forming thunderstorms, meteorologists look for moisture, instability, lift, and **wind shear** in the atmosphere. But these conditions do not guarantee tornadoes. "A large variety of weather patterns can lead to tornadoes; often, similar patterns may produce no severe weather at all," meteorologist Roger Edwards told the Storm Prediction Center web site.

As the weather gets closer, meteorologists watch out for one particular tell-tale sign—a rotating thunderstorm called a **supercell**. The **National Oceanic and Atmospheric Administration (NOAA)** web site reports: "These very intense thunderstorms are readily observed by radar and are used by NWS forecasters to issue tornado warnings. However, we are not yet able to distinguish between supercells that will and will not produce tornadoes."

Predicting tornadoes

Doppler radar is a key forecasting tool that measures the location, **precipitation**, direction, and wind speeds of a thunderstorm. It also detects the rotating winds that can create a tornado. The introduction of many Doppler radars into tornado-prone regions has contributed to the NWS's average tornado warning time of 13 minutes. Mobile Dopplers are attached to weather vans to take closer readings of tornadoes.

Despite the array of technological advances that replace the hand-plotted charts of 50 years ago, it takes human intervention to make sense of all the information and write it down in a clear form. "The most important hardware for forecasting at the Storm Prediction Center is the human hand. Numerous hand-drawn analyses of surface and upper-air data are still performed every day so forecasters can be intimately familiar with the weather features," says Roger Edwards.

A Doppler on Wheels truck, such as this one, was responsible for recording the extremely strong winds of the El Reno tornado.

Tornado countries

The United States experiences the largest numbers of tornadoes in the world, with around 1,250 reported every year. But tornadoes are not just a U.S. phenomenon—they occur on every continent except Antarctica. There is always the chance for the formation of thunderstorms if the conditions are favorable. It is no coincidence that tornadoes often form in places where cold polar air mixes with warm tropical air, such as in Tornado Alley. Interestingly, the places where tornadoes occur most frequently are also Earth's most fertile agricultural regions. This is because the rainfall associated with thunderstorms helps plants to grow.

Where tornadoes happen

It is difficult to estimate the number of tornadoes that happen globally every year, because they often go unreported. In Australia, around 20 tornadoes are reported annually, but many more are thought to occur in the desert outback, where there is nobody to see them. In the vast rural lands of Russia, many tornadoes are also unreported. The poorer country of Bangladesh has suffered from several violent tornadoes, but it lacks the observation networks to report every one that happens.

Tornado kingdom

Many people are surprised to learn that the country with the most tornadoes per land size is the United Kingdom. Around 33 tornadoes are reported in the United Kingdom every year, although most of them are too weak to cause major damage. Terence Meaden from the Tornado and Storm Research Organization (TORRO) said the area is susceptible to tornadoes because of its position on the Atlantic seaboard. It is here that cold air from the North Pole meets tropical air from the equator. "This is a region where there is often mixing of air, giving rise to the very unstable conditions that cause a tornado," Meaden told the *Guardian* newspaper.

The United Kingdom's largest tornado outbreak came on November 23, 1981, when 105 tornadoes formed over five and a half hours in a single area. Thirteen tornadoes were reported in Norfolk, England, alone. The deadliest tornado in UK history occurred on December 28, 1879, when two or three tornadoes destroyed the Tay Bridge in Dundee, Scotland. A passenger train crossing the bridge plunged into the Tay Estuary as a result, and 74 people were killed.

One country that has similar observational weather networks to the United States is Canada. Canada also has the second-highest number of tornadoes in the world, with 80 to 100 every year. Elsewhere, records show tornadoes have created major losses in Europe, India, Japan, and South America. Western Asia, New Zealand, and South Africa have reported frequent tornadoes, and China and Argentina have both been hit by rare, deadly tornadoes. However, the United States remains the one place most likely to be struck by tornadoes over EF3 in strength.

This 2006 tornado in London resulted in about 100 houses being damaged. But most tornadoes in the region are too weak to cause major damage.

DOSSIER:
THE DAULATPUR-SATURIA TORNADO

The Daulatpur–Saturia tornado, which struck Bangladesh in 1989, is the deadliest tornado on record. Although there is no official death toll, estimates place the number of dead at approximately 1,300. The tornado touched down at 6:30 p.m. on April 26, nearly 25 miles (40 kilometers) from the capital, Dhaka. It then cut a 10-mile (16-kilometer) path through the drought-stricken Daulatpur, Saturia, and Manikganj Sadar areas. The tornado destroyed everything in its path, including dried-out crops, trees, villages, and livestock. The heavy rain that followed the tornado obliterated any crops left standing.

The 1989 Bangladesh tornado flattened townships in the Manikganj area.

∨

CASUALTIES:	An estimated 1,300 dead, 12,000 injured, 80,000 people left homeless
DATE:	April 26, 1989
LOCAL TIME:	6:30 p.m.
PATH:	10 mi. (16 km)

BANGLADESH TORNADOES TIMELINE

APRIL 11, 1964
A violent tornado wipes out seven villages in the Mohammadpur region, killing over 500 people

APRIL 14, 1969
Two and possibly three devastating tornadoes strike central and eastern Bangladesh, killing over 920 people

APRIL 17, 1973
A tornado kills 681 people and levels eight villages in the Manikganj district

APRIL 26, 1989
The Daulatpur–Saturia tornado kills 1,300

MAY 13, 1996
An F2 tornado kills 700 people and delivers huge, baseball ball-sized hailstones

Recovery and Reconstruction

It is June 20 in Moore—one month since the tornado struck. The suburb is still continuing its massive cleanup operation. While the news cameras and international **media** have long since gone, Moore is a hive of activity. Inside the tornado zone, residents and volunteers dismantle the remains of homes and add the debris to the pile on the curb, where it is picked up by contractors.

"I'm just kind of looking back through [the debris], just to see if I could find anything maybe that I missed. I'm looking around, just all the trains that my kids had, the cars—all the little things like that. It's just hard to let it go sometimes," homeowner Matt Malone told Fox25 News.

Dark skies move on

"Everybody seems a little more encouraged this week than three weeks ago. Three weeks ago was pretty sad."

Glenn Lewis, Moore's mayor, speaking to Fox25 News

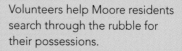

Volunteers help Moore residents search through the rubble for their possessions.

Big trucks

Alongside the volunteers, paid contractors were brought in from around the United States to help clean up. Some of the contractors drove trucks picking up loads of debris. Others documented and photographed on iPads what each load contained. This helped FEMA to calculate the cost of the cleanup.

By June 20, about 58,500 tons of debris has been cleared away, but there is an estimated 90,500 tons to go. The debris is the legacy of 1,248 buildings destroyed during the Oklahoma tornadoes. As a result, around 3,000 people have been left homeless in Moore. Barbara Garcia's home of 45 years was destroyed during the tornado. However, the news is not all bad. After Garcia was seen being reunited with her pet on CBS News, $61,000 was donated to help her rebuild her house. "Even though I've lost, I have gained so much. This has shown me how many good, good people are out there," Garcia told CBS News.

Volunteers fill the void

For the homeless residents of Moore, help came from many places. In June 2013, FEMA announced that $8 million in financial assistance had been paid to 11,000 tornado victims. The money was used to provide temporary housing, cover medical and funeral costs, and give unemployment payments to those who lost their jobs as a result of the tornado. There was also an influx of volunteers pouring into Moore. The volunteers did everything, from delivering Family Start Kits of towels, toothpaste, and **first-aid** supplies to homeless families to clearing away the debris. "We still have a lot of work to do, but you can see the progress made every day. They get to a point where they don't know what to do next, so we come in, do our little part, and give them a helping hand," Alabama volunteer Danny Hardy told KFOR-TV News.

Charities

While charities organized the volunteers flooding into Moore, they also worked behind the scenes, processing the millions of dollars the public had donated. Charities and other nonprofit organizations play an important role following natural disasters such as tornadoes. In Moore, they provided food, shelter, and essentials such as clothes, toiletries, and medicine to those affected.

As the emergency subsided, charities turned to Moore's long-term recovery: "The devastation is far-reaching in both human life and property…These impacted communities will take months or even years to recover," said Salvation Army Major Steve Morris.

Difficult donations

Charities depend on donations to operate, and people gave generously to help those in Moore. But the charities also received many items that were not needed, such as shoes, stuffed animals, and clothes. "We've had very few people that have even come and looked at clothes. The people who have lost their homes, many of them aren't even in a permanent **dwelling**. They don't have room for a closet full of clothes," Salvation Army spokeswoman Jennifer Dodd told the Huffington Post.

A homeless family picks up aid supplies from a parking lot in Moore.

Scammers and cash

Scammers started to take advantage of people's good will. Some pretended to collect for charities. Stephanie Cardwell of Colorado Springs, Colorado, said she was called by a scammer asking for money for the tornado victims. Cardwell smelled a rat. "I said, 'Would I get a tax letter with my donation?' And she didn't know anything about tax letters... I asked her if she had a 501(c)3 nonprofit number that she could give me. She didn't know anything about that either," Cardwell told KCCI8 News. Oklahoma Attorney General Scott Pruitt said 30 investigators were in the field helping Oklahomans to avoid scams.

At other times, donations could not get through. A Canadian refrigerated truck filled with almost 20,000 tons of food for Moore was stopped by officials at the U.S. border. It was unable to enter the United States until documentation was provided for every item. This is standard procedure to show something is not harmful or illegal in the United States, but much of the food spoiled as a result. Before long, charities asked people to send donations of money only.

Send in your money

Millions of dollars were donated to charities working in Moore. Within three days of the tornado, the Red Cross alone had raised $15 million. In addition, radio stations raised hundreds of thousands of dollars through on-air request-a-thons (people paying for their music requests to be played), U.S. businesses donated over $31.3 million in aid, and several concerts raised millions more.

A charity's perspective

"Monetary donations are the very best way to help. Your donations allow us to purchase supplies and relief items locally as well as to provide shelter, food, and emotional support to those in desperate need in Oklahoma."

Nigel Holderby, American Red Cross communications officer

DOSSIER:
THE BRIDGE CREEK-MOORE TORNADO

On May 3, 1999, the 100th tornado to strike the Oklahoma City area since 1890—and a tornado with the strongest winds ever recorded—touched down. The tornado raged across 38 miles (61 kilometers), devastating towns, killing 42 people, and caused about $1 billion in damages. The tornado was only one of a 74-tornado outbreak that struck the states of Kansas and Oklahoma over a 21-hour period. The outbreak resulted in a total of 48 fatalities, 800 injuries, 8,000 homes damaged or destroyed, and a total cost of almost $1.5 billion.

The line of the Bridge Creek-Moore tornado can be compared to its more recent counterparts in Moore.

A tornado takes its threatening black color from the dust, dirt, and debris it has sucked from the ground.

QUICK FACTS

CASUALTIES: 42 fatalities, 583 direct injuries, and immeasurable indirect injuries in Oklahoma City

WIND SPEED: Doppler on Wheels (DOW) radar recorded speeds of 301 mi. (484 km) per hour inside the tornado

TOTAL COST: $1 billion; the fourth-most expensive in history (the most expensive was the 2011 Joplin, Missouri, tornado, at $2.8 billion)

DAMAGE: 1,800 homes destroyed, 2,500 homes damaged

BRIDGE CREEK-MOORE TORNADO TIMELINE

4:47 p.m.
The NWS issues a tornado warning for western and central Oklahoma

5:41 p.m.
NWS Norman issues the following alert: The storms will be moving toward the Oklahoma City metropolitan area...very large hail and damaging winds...storms may also produce tornadoes

6:23 p.m.
A tornado touches down 2 mi. (3.2 km) southwest of Amber. It travels 6.5 mi. (10.6 km) to the Bridge Creek community and strikes with an F4/F5 intensity.

6:57 p.m.
The tornado moves across Interstate 44, west of Newcastle. NWS Norman issues a tornado emergency for south Oklahoma.

7:11 p.m.
The tornado weakens to an F2/F3 intensity as it crosses I-44 and the Canadian River near SW 149th Street

7:30 p.m.
The tornado regains F4/F5 intensity as it enters Moore, destroying 1,800 homes and damaging 2,500 others

7:48 p.m.
The tornado moves west of Moore and dissipates

What Have We Learned?

After the 2013 Moore tornado, a debate raged about the city's lack of storm shelters and safe rooms. Many were critical that Plaza Towers Elementary School did not have a safe area for shelter. Parent Echo Mackey huddled with her son in the school hallway when the tornado struck. "There's no question in my mind that that school was not safe enough," she told the *New York Times*. Seven students were killed at the school.

While the city of Moore's web site recommends "that every residence have a storm safe room or an underground cellar," there is no law requiring public buildings or homes to have them.

Types of shelter

There are three types of tornado shelter available in the United States:
1. An outside, underground **storm cellar**
2. A home safe room, built like a reinforced concrete closet
3. Large community shelters, which can fit dozens of people inside.

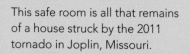

This safe room is all that remains of a house struck by the 2011 tornado in Joplin, Missouri.

Following the devastating Moore tornado of 1999, the state of Oklahoma made $12 million available to help people build safe rooms. But despite this government money, only around 10 percent of homes in Moore have a storm shelter or safe room. For many people, even with financial assistance, the cost is too high. Moore builder Curtis McCarty told the *New York Times* that a small, closet-sized safe room costs around $3,000. "Another three or four thousand dollars on every new home can really add up when you're trying to keep houses affordable," McCarty said.

But Moore resident Jennifer Walker, who lost her home in the tornado, said she would find a way to pay for this next time. "Oh yeah, I would forego the granite whirlpool tub. I would forego all that just to have the shelter, for sure," she told the Associated Press.

Lessons learned

Every tornado teaches us something more about them. The following points can all be taken from the 2013 Oklahoma tornadoes:

- Tornadoes can strike anywhere at anytime, if the conditions are right.
- Tornadoes can strike the same place twice—or more. In the last 14 years, Moore has suffered from two EF5 tornadoes and one EF4.
- Tornadoes are unpredictable. The El Reno tornado killed three veteran storm chasers who were taken by surprise when the tornado changed its path.
- Never try to outrun a tornado. Many people trying to drive away from the El Reno tornado ended up trapped in gridlocked traffic as the tornado approached.
- Pay attention to alerts. The NWS's tornado watches, warnings, and emergencies gave Moore residents enough time to take shelter and saved countless lives.
- Don't believe everything that is reported. Television, the Internet, and social media mean news travels faster than ever, even if it is incorrect.
- We are still learning. Many questions about tornadoes are still unanswered, but research by scientists and meteorologists is helping us better understand them.
- Have a plan. Knowing in advance where to take shelter and what to do when a tornado strikes can save your life.

Timeline

May 13, 2013 The NWS's Storm Prediction Center in Norman, Oklahoma, issues a severe weather outlook for the central United States

May 15-17 A weather system accompanied by thunderstorms, damaging winds, and hail reaches Colorado, Kansas, and Nebraska. Twenty-one tornadoes touch down in Texas, including an EF4 tornado that kills six people.

May 18 The NWS issues tornado watches for Nebraska, Kansas, and Colorado. Twenty-four tornadoes are reported, including an EF4 in Rozel, Kansas.

May 19 Ten tornadoes touch down in Kansas and several more in Oklahoma, including an EF4, which kills two people in the town of Shawnee

May 20 The NWS issues a tornado watch for Oklahoma. Between 2:56 p.m. and 3:35 p.m., a tornado reaching EF5 in strength destroys homes and buildings in Moore and leaves 24 people dead.

May 21 Search and rescue teams pull over 100 survivors from ruined buildings and homes in Moore. Survey teams from the NWS investigate the tornado damage. Charities, government officials, and news crews enter Moore to help survivors, assess the damage, and report the news.

May 22-26 The cleanup begins in Moore as severe winds cause widespread damage across Michigan, Massachusetts, Oklahoma, Tennessee, eastern Kentucky, New York, New Hampshire, and Canada. No tornadoes are reported.

May 26-30	Multiple tornadoes touch down across the Great Plains, causing severe damage in Kansas, Nebraska, Michigan, and Oklahoma
May 31	The widest EF5 tornado in U.S. history, with the second-highest winds recorded on Earth, strikes El Reno, Oklahoma. Nine people are killed. There is controversy when residents try to outrun the tornado, which causes widespread congestion on local highways and roads.
June 1	Oklahoma Governor Mary Fallin inspects the damage in El Reno. Those left homeless are provided with specially converted shipping containers to live in.
June 20	The long cleanup continues in Moore. Many of the 3,000 people left homeless rely on charity and government handouts to survive.

Glossary

amateur somebody who does something for enjoyment, rather than being paid for it

debris scattered pieces of solid material left over after something has been destroyed

dissipate disappear into nothing

donation money or a gift, often given to a charity to help those in need

Doppler radar tracking machine that uses radar to determine the location, strength, precipitation, and wind speed of a tornado

dwelling house, apartment, or any other structure where people live

Enhanced Fujita Scale scale used in the United States and Canada to rate tornadoes based on the amount of damage they cause

Federal Emergency Management Agency (FEMA) U.S. government agency that helps people before and after disasters

first aid medical help given to injured people

first responder medically trained emergency service worker (fire, police, medical, or other) who is among the first on the scene at an emergency or disaster

flash flood sudden rush of water, often destructive to anything in its path, caused by heavy rainfall

foundation stone or concrete structure that sits below a building to support it

funnel spiral-shaped center of a tornado

Great Plains area of flat, prairie land in North America, which lies east of the Rocky Mountains and west of the Mississippi River

gridlock traffic jam in which no vehicle can move in any direction

hurricane clip steel clip that connects the roof of a building to its main structure, used to protect against high winds

hypothermia condition in which the body temperature falls below normal

interstate highway connecting two U.S. states

media radio, television, newspapers, magazines, and the Internet

meteorologist scientist who studies the weather

National Guard volunteer soldiers who serve each U.S. state in times of emergency and war

National Oceanic and Atmospheric Administration (NOAA) U.S. agency focused on the condition of the oceans and the atmosphere. It is the NOAA's job to warn the public of dangerous weather, through its NWS department.

National Severe Storms Laboratory (NSSL) NOAA weather laboratory that investigates severe weather. NSSL scientists were responsible for developing the first Doppler radar.

National Weather Service (NWS) part of the NOAA that provides forecasts and weather warnings to the public

news anchor person who reports the TV news and is often very well known

observation network any meteorological system that watches the weather, including weather satellites, weather balloons, and weather stations

precipitation any form of solid or liquid water that falls from a cloud, including rain, snow, sleet, and hail

radar device that uses radio waves to detect and locate an object and find its position and speed

safe room room in a house that can withstand an assault. Tornado safe rooms are often the size of a closet or larger and are built from steel and reinforced concrete.

satellite small, unmanned spacecraft that orbits Earth and gathers weather information to send back to Earth

search and rescue team group of people, and often dogs, who locate and rescue those who are trapped in confined spaces, usually as a result of a disaster

shelter either the place that gives protection from storms or the act of hiding in that place

shrapnel small objects or broken fragments that can injure people or animals when thrown out by an explosion or high-speed winds

storm cellar room often built under a house or in the yard nearby, where people can take shelter during a disaster such as a tornado

Storm Prediction Center (SPC) provides forecasts for the risk of severe thunderstorms and tornadoes in the United States. It is responsible for alerting the public to approaching tornadoes through tornado watches, warnings, and emergencies. The SPC is part of the NWS.

storm siren loud siren that warns people of approaching danger, such as a tornado. It is also known as an air raid siren.

supercell huge, rotating storm cloud that can create damaging hail, severe winds, lightning, flash floods, and tornadoes

surreal bizarre, weird

tetanus serious infection caused by the harmful bacteria *Clostridium tetani* entering a wound

tri-state territory made up of three adjoining states

volatile sudden and unpredictable change

volunteer person who carries out work without being paid for it

weather radio special radio that picks up high-frequency weather broadcasts during times of extreme weather

wind shear major change in wind speed and direction over a short distance

Find Out More

Books

Burnie, David. *Disasters* (Scholastic Discover More). New York: Scholastic, 2013.

Green, Jen. *Surviving Natural Disasters* (Real Life Heroes). Mankato, Minn.: Arcturus, 2010.

Jeffrey, Gary. *Tornadoes and Superstorms* (Graphic Natural Disasters). New York: Rosen, 2007.

Raum, Elizabeth. *Surviving Tornadoes* (Children's True Stories). Chicago: Raintree, 2012.

Rooney, Anne. *Responding to Emergencies* (Charities in Action). Chicago: Heinemann Library, 2013.

Royston, Angela. *Storms* (Eyewitness Disaster). New York: Marshall Cavendish Benchmark, 2011.

Schneider, Bonnie. *Extreme Weather*. New York: Palgrave Macmillan, 2012.

Stiefel, Chana. *Forces of Nature*. New York: Scholastic, 2010.

Web sites

www.defense.gov/home/features/2013/0513_oktornadoes
This U.S. Department of Defense web site gives specific information on the 2013 Oklahoma tornadoes.

emergency.cdc.gov/disasters/tornadoes/prepared.asp
This web site gives advice on how to prepare for a tornado.

news.discovery.com/earth/tags/tornado.html
This is the Discovery Channel's web site, which provides recent articles and information on tornadoes.

www.nssl.noaa.gov/education/svrwx101/tornadoes
This web site for the NSSL gives facts about tornadoes and current tornado research.

www.ready.gov/kids-old/know-facts
This is a good FEMA site for younger readers because it gives short definitions of all natural disasters.

video.nationalgeographic.com/video/environment/environment-natural-disasters/tornadoes/tornadoes-101/
This interesting video gives you a basic overview of tornadoes.

www.weatherwizkids.com/weather-tornado.htm
This web site is dedicated to teaching younger readers about all types of weather, including tornadoes.

More topics to research

1. Find out more about charities such as the Red Cross (www.redcross.org) or the Salvation Army (salvationarmyusa.org).

2. Find out more about tornadoes on water, which are called waterspouts (oceanservice.noaa.gov/facts/waterspout.html).

3. Find out more about how to prepare for other natural disasters (emergency.cdc.gov/disasters).

4. Watch current natural disasters and extreme weather systems from NASA space satellites at: earthobservatory.nasa.gov/NaturalHazards.

5. Find out about Texas Tech University's safe room and storm shelter development at: www.depts.ttu.edu/nwi/research/shelters.php.

Index